In The Same Way, Teach...
To Lead a Holy Life

Elaine Oostra

13-Session Bible Study on Titus 2:1-5

Unless otherwise indicated, all Scripture quotations are taken from HOLY BIBLE ENGLISH STANDARD VERSION

Copyright 2017 by Elaine Oostra
Published by Field of View Press
Parma, Idaho

Cover designed by Elaine Oostra
Edited by JoEllen Claypool and Jan Neashum and Sandra Koivisto

Printed and bound in the United Stated of America. All rights reserved. No part of this publication may be reproduced or transmitted in any form or by any means, electronic, mechanical, or digital including photocopying, recording, or by an information storage and retrieval system - except by a reviewer who may quote brief passages and in a review to be printed in a newspaper, magazine, or by the web – without permission in writing from this publisher.

For more information or additional copies please contact:
Field of View Press
P.O. Box 1087
Parma, Idaho
fieldofviewpress@gmail.com

First printing 2017

ISBN: 978-0-9972316-1-8

Library of Congress Control Number – 2017905307

TABLE OF CONTENTS

	Foreword	v
	A Personal Word From Elaine	vii
	Introduction	1
Lesson 1	Insecure vs Secure	5
Lesson 2	Being Confident	13
Lesson 3	Knowing Truth – Sound Doctrine	17
Lesson 4	Godly Living	25
Lesson 5	Renounce Ungodliness	33
Lesson 6	Meaning of Love – Storge - Eros	37
Lesson 7	Such Were Some of You	45
Lesson 8	Meaning of Love – Phileo - Agape	53
Lesson 9	Pattern for Marriage	59
Lesson 10	Marriage as a Covenant	65
Lesson 11	Self-Control	71
Lesson 12	Submission	77
Lesson 13	Honor God With Our Lives	85
	Role Models	93
	Titus 2:1-8	105

The picture on the front cover is one on the many trails my dear friend and I used to run on almost every day. We would meet at Berthusen Park before the sun was up, rain or shine. During our runs, we would pray for our husbands and our children. In 1999 she went home to be with Jesus. ALS (Lou Gehrig's disease) took her body but not her soul. I share more of my dear friend in my book, *One Brick at a Time*. The path in this picture reminds me of Jesus being the one and only way to the Father. I am to walk in a way where my life reflects Jesus Christ.

FOREWORD
In the Same Way, Teach …

Elaine has been my mentor for 22 years, and when she asked me to go through this study and write the foreword, I was honored to. I am in a unique position as a 38-year-old woman. I am sometimes the older woman, as well as being the younger woman depending on what situation I'm in. The important thing I remind myself of is that I am a woman called by God to be a wife, mom, daughter, sister, and friend. I have many opportunities throughout my day to be an example for younger women and learn from older and younger women alike.

Elaine's study, *In the Same Way, Teach …*, starts off with her challenging us. She says, "I want to be an example and teach those younger than me. Do you have the desire to do that too? If we don't teach them, the world will. Let's learn and see how we can be examples and how we can teach the younger women." Elaine's challenge is very relevant to us today, as we can see in many media platforms the decline of our society and the wandering away from God's laws and His Word. It is of utmost importance and with a profound sense of urgency that we need to rise to our calling to teach those younger than us. This study will equip you to do just that, and Elaine starts off by teaching us about who God says we are in Him. We cannot teach what we have not ourselves experienced, at least not effectively. Elaine brings us from who we are in Christ to what He has called us to be by taking us through scriptures that are challenging and require one to honestly search their heart to know if they are on the right path. I would encourage you to be open to this process and in turn *"be doers of the word, and not hearers only"* (English Standard Version, James 1:22a).

In the Same Way, Teach … is full of verses of God's truth, and Elaine does a wonderful job of walking you through them all. These Scriptures are a guided tour of what God has called us as older women to be, and are an encouragement to walk in that calling. My prayer is that you would not go through this study for the sake of doing another study, but that you would be encouraged and have confidence to walk in that which God has called you to. *"For we are His workmanship, created in Christ Jesus for good works, which God prepared beforehand, that we should walk in them"* (ESV, Ephesians 2:10).

May God pour out His blessings upon you as you work through this study, and I pray you would trust Him as He leads you in this way, to teach the younger women.

Your sister in Christ Jesus,

Emma Swinburnson

A PERSONAL WORD FROM ELAINE

The reason for my writing this particular study to teach younger women, was because of an older women in my life named Barb. She mentored me without even knowing it. This was a life changing experience for me. It was how God taught me that He could use us wherever we are!

One day, I was getting my hair foiled. Yep, that's tin foil all over my head that somehow holds the color product. What some of us won't go through to cover those gray hairs we are not ready to show to the world yet. Vain, I know!

In walked a young man who had been in my youth group several years before. It was so embarrassing. I don't know about you, but this women doesn't like others, especially males, seeing this sight that looks like an antenna had blown up on my head. Being held captive by my hair with no way to escape! He sat down, not understanding how awkward this was for me. Finally, I told him I didn't like him seeing me like that. He replied back that it didn't matter to him. *Ok*, I thought, *get over yourself.*

As we started to chat it became clear how much he needed to talk about issues in his life. He trusted the hairdresser and me with his heart. At one point, I even told him to tell me to be quiet if he didn't want to hear what was being said. He said, "No, I want to hear what you have to say." This showed me how badly he was hurting.

It amazes me to think while sitting in a beauty shop chair it was possible to minister to the young man. He left later with the encouragement to love his wife unconditionally as Christ loved him.

The next morning, I was thanking my Father in Heaven for bringing me to this little town that I had never heard of before. Pondering the opportunity God had given to me while getting my hair cut. My thoughts immediately went to an amazing women God had placed in my life and all I had learned from her.

When we moved to Parma, if wasn't easy to leave my family and a dear friend who had known me so well. It was leaving my security of everything and everyone I knew. Making new friends is not easy for me and that is why I had prayed for God to bring friends into my life to bring me this same kind of comfort.

The first Sunday we showed up at the new church, sitting in front of me was a women who when she turned around to greet me her face was lit up and radiating Christ. Barb then grabbed my hand to welcome me. It was at that moment I knew that I wanted to get to know her better.

Before God bought Barb into my life, the thought of ministering to other people was such a scary thought to me. It was easier in a safe environment like church. Being with her and watching in amazement how she reached out to people anywhere opened my eyes and heart. She would take strangers into her home, feeding them and at the same time serving them.. Through her, I met people who would never have crossed my path in life. At the same time it became clear how selfish a person I was . Yet, Barb cared about other people's lives and what got them into their particular situations. She listened! She loved unconditionally.

From the time spent with her, God was teaching me and causing me to grow.

In Titus 2:3:5 the older women are instructed to teach the younger women. My desire is for God to use you and me as older women to teach the younger. In watching Barb, it gave me more of a desire to be able to minister as she did. Sometimes I would joke and say, " when I grow up I want to be like Barb." Oh, that all of us older women would have the desire to be a Godly example to the younger women today.

We had our differences in some biblical nonessentials but in the essentials, we totally agreed. She has always shown me unconditional love. Barb knew my struggles in life and was a big part of my healing process. There wasn't anything I couldn't tell her and have her be shocked. She would say, "We need to pray about this." And we did. She was a huge encourager, being with me step by step in the healing process of my past pain. God used her mightily in my life and it's made me spiritually stronger.

Barb and her husband moved miles away to be with their grandkids, a dream come true for her. For me has been like a bird kicked out of the nest learning to fly on her own. But that is a good thing.

Thank you, Barb, for the Jesus Christ I saw in you! I still have so much to learn in ministering to others. Even when having an explosion of tin foil on my head! God knew when I moved 580 miles from my birth place that you would be the older woman needed to mentor me. Yes, there have been others too, but I know my life would not be the same today without having you in it. I love you Barb!

Elaine Oostra

INTRODUCTION

For 20 years I have studied the Bible inductively through Precept Ministries, an in-depth Bible study class. God has prepared me, and still is preparing me, for that which He has purposed for me. God has prepared me to be a Berean where I am challenged to search the Scriptures when others speak (see Acts 17:10-11). The Bereans only had the Old Testament to use in order to verify whether the words Paul and Silas were speaking were true. They checked the prophecies that were fulfilled through Yeshua.

To be a Berean, you need to read, check, and examine whether what I am saying is actually true. Bereans are not gullible to the extent of accepting anything that is taught to them. They search the Scriptures daily. Today, we are content to accept most anything. *"Beloved, believe not every spirit, but try the spirits whether they are of God: because many false prophets are gone out into the world"* (King James Version, I John 4:1).

For well over a decade I have been leading Bible studies with high school girls and wrote my own curriculum most of the time. We can't be lazy in studying the Word of God and neglect preparing our lesson. In doing so, we teach the younger women to be neglectful and careless with God's Word. Be a Berean!

In teaching these girls, I pick a biblical topic or a book of the Bible. I print out Bible passages and have the girls mark words; this teaches them to look at what that particular Scripture verse is saying to us using it in the context of the rest of Scripture. This study is an accumulation of what I have taught younger women. I am hoping this Bible study will encourage other ladies to become Bereans and teach the younger women correct teachings.

I want to share with you, as "older women" (meaning "mature Christian women"), that the teens today have the same emotions and struggles we did umpteen years ago. However, I have noticed the pressure on them is WAY stronger than 40 years ago.

Each one of these girls that has come into my home is searching for her worth. I am amazed at their answers when I ask them what they struggle with the most. The majority of the girls struggle with their body shape, if they are pretty enough, or if they are smart enough.

I have been where they are! If I could now see myself at age 16, I think I would see my body with different eyes. It would be wrinkle free with no effects of gravity that are now dragging body parts downward! But the sad truth is I still would not be content today if that's all I had to make myself feel acceptable to others.

Standing in the grocery line for me is torture. I have magazines on both sides of me with a woman my age on the front cover in a bikini, a board-flat stomach and not a wrinkle in sight. I want to tell women around me, "This is not real. Please, let's not measure ourselves by this picture!" Instead, I look around me to see if anyone can see what I am about to do. Sneakily, I put the magazines behind the cooking magazine.

At another store, I saw magazines displayed on a table with a barely dressed-teen girl sitting on an old Santa's lap. I took them and hid them under the table. I was sure that the young people working behind the busy counter would not have done anything if I told them of my opinion of the display.

It saddens me to see women my age give in to the pressure of using silicone, or whatever they use today, to put body parts back where they used to be or getting liposuction in an attempt to get the perfect shape. Is this the example we are giving those younger than us, that you have to look perfect in order to be acceptable to others and yourself! Yikes! Ladies, our identity cannot be found in the perkiness of our body parts!

Ladies, we have a responsibility as 'older' women to teach the younger women. *"They are to teach what is good, and so train young women to love their husbands and their children"* (English Standard Version, Titus 2:3b – 4).

I also pray that younger women will have the heart to learn from the older women. I pray God takes any pride from their hearts and opens them up to learn. *"Therefore encourage one another and build one another up, just as you are doing"* (ESV, I Thessalonians 5:11).

The Bible tells us to, *"be prepared to give an answer"* (New International Version, I Peter 3:15). *"Preach the word; be ready in season and out of season; reprove, rebuke, and exhort, with complete patience and teaching"* (English Standard Version, II Timothy 4:2).

When I teach teen girls, trust me, I learn from them also. I remember the strain of being a teen. I hear how the world is pressing in on them even more than my ancient of days ago of being a teen. I see them as diamonds in the rough and encourage them to hang in there and that God will use their hardships for His purpose.

Ministering to young moms can once again remind us of what it felt like to have a little one hanging on us all day long and of little fingers wiggling under the bathroom door that demanded our attention. Conversations with them help us to recall the days we felt like pulling our hair out and just wanting to talk to another adult. We desired to use grown-up language, like, "I need to use the restroom" instead of, "I need to go potty." (I have reverted to using that word as a grandma.)

As older women, we need to minister to a mom who is exasperated at what happened to her adorable child that now is a teen and seems to have switched places with someone from another planet. We need to encourage the moms whose young adult children have denounced God or whose child still believes but has walked away from everything their parents lovingly instilled in them. Have your heart and mind open to whomever God wants you to minister to and encourage.

Before we start the study in the book of Titus chapter two, I want us as mature women to understand where we can find true security and confidence. It helps our heart and our mind to be more open to what God wants to teach us. In Titus, we will learn how to be godly, strong women when we live according to God's calling on our lives.

LESSON 1
INSECURE VS SECURE

How we present ourselves as women physically, being younger or older in age, says a lot about our relationship with Jesus Christ.

What message are we sending to those women who are younger than us? Are we passing on a legacy of being secure in Christ? Or are we passing on insecurity by being so focused on self that all our time, money and energy is spent on ourselves to the point that we don't minister to others? Could we be narcissistic? It seems we, as women, can go from one extreme to another. We either think our bodies need to be perfect which, by the way, is unrealistic or we think we have to be covered from head to toe.

Narcissistic (adjective)
1. having an undue fascination with oneself; vain
2. Psychoanalysis; tending to derive erotic gratification from admiration of one's own physical or mental attributes

---

There are women in the Bible that were called beautiful. Kings even noticed their beauty. *"The young woman had a beautiful figure and was lovely to look at"* (ESV,

Esther 2:7b). We know Esther had more than her outward beauty, *"Now Esther was winning favor in the eyes of all who saw her"* (ESV, Esther 2:15b). I believe Esther had an inner beauty that made her outward beauty shine.

It may have been it was a common practice for that era for most women to get a year of beauty treatment before their wedding? They did, *"six months with oil of myrrh and six months with spices and ointment for women"* (ESV, Esther 2:12b). Can we bring that tradition back even if it was only for royalty?

Let's look at what the Bible does says about women and our appearance.

"Likewise also that women should adorn themselves in respectable apparel, with modesty and self-control, not with braided hair and gold or pearls or costly attire, but with what is proper for women who profess godliness-with good works" (ESV, I Timothy 2:9-10).

This verse is not saying it's wrong to wear jewelry or cute clothes or to get our hair done. We just can't let it become an obsession in our lives. The New Living Translation says in verse 9b, *"They should wear decent and appropriate clothing and not draw attention to themselves."*

According to I Timothy 2:9-10, what should draw others to us?

How can we make ourselves attractive by the things we do or how we present ourselves?

I have a dear friend who has an hourglass-shaped body, and she has struggled with weight all of her life. The world would never call her "attractive", but to me, she screams the word B-E-A-U-T-I-F-U-L! Oh yes, she colors her hair too, and she is in her seventies! She wears the cutest clothes for her body shape. Her husband adores her. But these are not the things that drew me to love her. She wore the attractiveness of Christ; she beams with His glory and love! She is the 'older' woman in my life, amongst many others I know and admire. They challenge me to be an older woman like them! They have been wonderful, godly examples to me.

God told us in Psalm 139 how He created us and that we are fearfully and wonderfully made. Honestly, ladies, do we see ourselves as wonderfully made? Many women suffer from insecurity. It's one of the enemy's (Satan) fiery darts he likes to throw at us. Let's, as women, learn how to stop insecure feelings. That is where in this lesson we will begin.

The meaning of insecure is interesting.

> **In.se.cure** ADJECTIVE (of a person) not confident or assured; uncertain and anxious.

Now let's look at the meaning of confidence.

> **Confidence -** The chief Hebrew word translated "confidence" (baTach, and its forms) means, perhaps, radically, "to be open," showing thus what originated the idea of "confidence"; where there was nothing hidden a person felt safe; it is very frequently rendered "trust."

Did you see that? It's the opposite of insecure! So when you say you are 'just insecure', you are telling others that you are not confident!

When we are feeling insecure, how can we know what it looks like to attain true security? Look up the following verses. What do they say in regards to security?

Jude 24

John 3:16

Ephesians 2:8-9

John 14:6

I Timothy 6:17

Jeremiah 17:7-8

Psalm 9:10

Deuteronomy 31:8

Lamentations 3:57

Matthew 6:31-34

Philippians 4:19

Isaiah 26:3

Summarize what you have learned through reading these Scripture verses regarding being secure.

Who supplies all your needs? (Philippians 4:19)

When we struggle with feelings of insecurity (and yes, we still will at times), who do we need to trust?

What happens when we stay in our insecurity and miss the peace of God?

How does this affect the ability to minister to the younger women?

Who wants to keep you insecure? Read I Peter 5:8 and Ephesians 6:10-18.

What can we do? (James 4:7)

Can you think of an example from your life that you can share with someone regarding how you are learning to trust God?

How can you encourage others of your security in how God made you, physically and your personality?

While doing a study called *Believing God* by Beth Moore, one thing from this study that became imprinted on my mind and heart was, "God is who He says He is, and I am who He says I am." I finally got it!

My question to you is, do you know who you are in Christ as an older, mature woman?

It is my desire to be an example and teach those younger than me. Do you have the desire to do that too? If we don't teach them, the world will. Let's look at how we can be examples and how we can teach the younger women.

Remember I am who Christ says I am. The security and confidence you and I need to walk in is in Christ.

The job of a mature Christian woman is to teach these young women where to go to find real worth and not self-worth. There is nothing in "self" that is worthy. It's only Christ in us that makes us worthy. Period.

It has to start with you and me as the mature women described in Titus chapter two. As you read, highlight words that stand out to you. I love words and the study of them. I encourage you to look up and compare the Scripture given in the other Bible versions which use other words to describe the same thing. It sometimes can help make the passage clearer. I am also going to have you look up different Scriptures so as to not take words out of context. Scripture supports Scripture. You will be taken on a few rabbit trails.

There will be a 🐰 at the beginning of the trail and a 🐰 at the end of the trail. Trust me, it all ties together. So hang in there with me! I promise you, this is the best beauty treatment you will ever have! We want people to approach us when you are standing in a line for coffee and say, "You're a Christian aren't you!" (It happen to me! I want it to happen again.) I want others to see how we radiate Jesus Christ more than they notice our cute outfit or new hair color.

Now let's take the time to get into God's Word and learn what God called women to do. In this way, you will be teach younger women.

LESSON 2
BEING CONFIDENT

*"Paul, a servant of God and an apostle of Jesus Christ, for the sake of the faith of God's elect and their knowledge of the truth, which accords with godliness, ² **in hope of eternal life,** which God, who never lies, promised before the ages began ³ and at the proper time manifested in his word through the preaching with which I have been entrusted by the command of God our Savior;*

⁴ To Titus, my true child in a common faith:

Grace and peace from God the Father and Christ Jesus our Savior" (ESV, Titus 1:1-4).

Paul was sent to proclaim faith to those whom God had chosen and to teach them to know the truth. This truth will show God's people how to live godly lives. But most of all, this truth gives <u>confidence</u>, *in hope of eternal life.*

It wasn't until the age of 28 that I was saved, born again, while reading the book of John. The Holy Spirit made it clear to me that Jesus died for me, a sinner. I received the security and <u>confidence</u> that I was a child of the living God. Before, I had felt so unworthy of God's love. <u>Confidence</u> cannot come to us any other way, no matter how hard we try, or how educated we are, or how wealthy and successful we become.

Confidence comes only through Jesus Christ," *I am the way, and the truth, and the life. No one comes to the Father except through me"* (ESV, John 14:6).

"In the fear of the LORD one has strong confidence, and his children will have a refuge" (ESV, Proverbs 14:26).

If we, as mature women, are secure in our relationship with Christ, how can this be a refuge to others we teach?

What influence could we have on others?

*"Such is the confidence that we have through Christ toward God. Not that we are **sufficient** in ourselves to claim anything as coming from us, but our **sufficiency** is from God, who has made us sufficient to be ministers of a new covenant, not of the letter but of the Spirit. For the letter kills, but the Spirit gives life"* (ESV, II Corinthians 3:4-6).

If we trust in God through Christ, what can we have?

How do we attain sufficiency?

Can we do anything of lasting value by ourselves?

Who made us competent to minister to others?

When we minister to young women, it has to be God working in us, not our own efforts. In the verses below, circle where your *confidence* comes from and underline what you are to do.

Ephesians 3:11-12, "*This was according to the eternal purpose that he has realized in Christ Jesus our Lord, ¹² in whom we have boldness and access with confidence through our faith in him*".

Hebrews 3:6, "*Christ is faithful over God's house as a son. And we are his house, if indeed we hold fast our confidence and our boasting in our hope.*"

Hebrews 3:14, "*For we have come to share in Christ, if indeed we hold our original confidence firm to the end.*"

Hebrews 4:16, "*Let us then with confidence draw near to the throne of grace, that we may receive mercy and find grace to help in time of need.*"

I John 4:16-17, "*So we have come to know and to believe the love that God has for us. God is love, and whoever abides in love abides in God, and God abides in him. By this is love perfected with us, so that we may have confidence for the day of judgment, because as he is so also are we in this world.*"

I John 5:14, "*And this is the confidence that we have toward him, that if we ask anything according to his will he hears us.*"

Hebrews 10:32-36, "*But recall the former days when, after you were enlightened, you endured a hard struggle with sufferings, sometimes being publicly exposed to reproach and affliction, and sometimes being partners with those so treated. For you had compassion on those in prison, and you joyfully accepted the plundering of your property, since you knew that you yourselves had a better possession and an abiding one. Therefore do not throw away your confidence, which has a great reward. For you have need of endurance, so that when you have done the will of God you may receive what is promised."*

Hebrews 10:17-22, *"then he adds, 'I will remember their sins and their lawless deeds no more.' Where there is forgiveness of these, there is no longer any offering for sin. Therefore, brothers, since we have confidence to enter the holy places by the blood of Jesus, by the new and living way that he opened for us through the curtain, that is, through his flesh, and since we have a great priest over the house of God, let us draw near with a true heart in full assurance of faith, with our hearts sprinkled clean from an evil conscience and our bodies washed with pure water."*

In looking at these verses, how does confidence from Christ play out as older women teaching the younger? How important is this?

If you are like me, you are growing daily, minute by minute really, in who you are in Christ! Please, don't grow weary in thinking you can never teach or be an influence in a younger woman's life. Many women have no idea how they encourage me. I silently watched mothers with older children when I was raising my family. I listened and watched how they disciplined. I saw how talking to your child in a controlled voice worked better than yelling, something I battled with as a young mom. I saw these older moms struggle in parenting, just like I did. I heard them encourage each other and admit their mistakes.

Our behavior and actions as older women matter. We are being observed. I am going to talk more about this later.

LESSON 3
KNOWING TRUTH – SOUND DOCTRINE

*"But as for you, teach what accords with **sound doctrine**."* (ESV, Titus 2:1).

As mature women, before we can teach the younger women, we need to **have true biblical knowledge.** Who better to teach what God's Word has to say than a mature, godly woman who has sound doctrine (teaching). I cannot sufficiently stress enough that sound doctrine is not happening today! Some are no longer teaching God's truths. They prefer to teach man's interpretation of the Bible according to popular cultural trends. Teens are getting confused by the mixed messages. They read the Bible, then they hear a pastor or teacher say the opposite of what the Bible is saying.

In chapter two, Paul instructs Titus to promote living godly lives because this reflects true teaching of God's Word. (See Titus 2:1b knowledge of truth, which accords with godliness.) Paul tells Titus in chapter 2 verse 3 what the older women are to be. He then instructs us in what we are to do and what we are to teach younger women and why we are to teach. In each chapter of this study, we are going to dive into the depth of the words that I put in bold print from Titus 2 at the beginning of the chapter.

But what is sound doctrine? It is instruction. Doctrine is teaching imparted by an authoritative source. Biblical doctrine helps us to understand God's will for our lives.

Titus 2:1-5, *"But as for you, teach what accords with sound doctrine. 2 Older men are to be sober-minded, dignified, self-controlled, sound in faith, in love, and in steadfastness.*

3 Older women likewise are to be reverent in behavior, not slanderers or slaves to much wine. They are to teach what is good,

4 and so train the young women to love their husbands and children,

5 to be self-controlled, pure, working at home, kind, and submissive to their own husbands, that the word of God may not be reviled."

Ladies, we are in a spiritual battle! We need to understand what God has called us to do. So let's get to work!

In Titus 2:1, what are we told to do?

Godly living reflects correct teaching. See Titus 1:1-2. Let this sink in. How does Titus 2:1-5 support this statement?

We need to be sound in our doctrine. What happens if we cause others to sin? What are the consequences for teaching false doctrine? (Mark 9:42)

If we don't have correct biblical doctrine, how can we get God's truth for our lives?

The meaning of Truth:

*Sound'ness,n.

Wholeness; entireness; an unbroken, unimpaired or undecayed state; as the soundness of timber, of fruit, of the teeth, of a limb. Firmness; strength; solidity; truth; as soundness of reasoning or argument, of doctrine or principles. Truth; rectitude; firmness; freedom from error or fallacy; orthodoxy; as soundness of faith. Sound, founded in truth; firm; strong; valid; solid; that cannot be overthrown or refuted; as sound reasoning; a sound reasoning; a sound objection; sound doctrine; sound principle. Right; correct; well founded; free from error; orthodox. II Timothy 1. Let my heart be sound in the statutes. Psalm 119

Read II Timothy 3:16. Who is our source and how much of the Scripture is inspired by this source?

For what is it useful?

What does Scripture teach us about our lives?

How does it help us and change us?

Below are two separate columns: one for those who hold to God's truth and what they do, and one for those who do not endure sound doctrine. Write down what the people do in the category they fit into.

	Sound Doctrine (True teaching)	**Not Sound Doctrine** (False teaching)
Titus 1:9 (example)	*Hold firmly, give instruction, rebuke those who contradict.*	*Contradict sound doctrine*
Titus 2:1		
II Timothy 4:2-4		
I Timothy 6:3-5		
II Peter 1:20-21		
II Timothy 3:5		
I Timothy 1:3		
II Timothy 1:13		
I John 4:1		

We are to teach what accords with sound doctrine. From the verses in the chart, what is God saying about sound doctrine and what does He want you and me to do with it?

What are we called if we interpret and teach God's Word to fit what we want it to say?

"Keep a close watch on yourself and on the teaching. Persist in this, for by so doing you will save both yourself and your hearers" (ESV, I Timothy 4:16).

What is the warning to us, as teachers, regarding what we present as truth?

Read I Timothy 1:1-11 to get the context.

Read I Timothy 1:5, 8-10. What happens to a person when they receive true doctrine (vs. 5 and 8)?

According to I Timothy 1:1-10, what is the warning about false teaching? What do they do with sound doctrine?

Read Ephesians 6:14. Where are we to stand firm?

In other words, true teaching promotes righteousness; sin flourishes where "the sound doctrine" is opposed. Again, **Godly living reflects right teaching.**

How easily can we lead someone astray when we don't know or understand the authority in which God speaks?

Sound doctrine is important because what we believe affects what we do with God's Word. Study the Word of God for yourselves. *"Do your best to present yourself to God as one approved, a worker who has no need to be ashamed, rightly handling the word of truth"* (ESV, II Timothy 2:15).

What happens if we do lead others into error? Again this is what Jesus tells us in Mark 9:42 *"Whoever causes one of these little ones who believe in me to sin, it would be better for him if a great millstone were hung around his neck and he were thrown into the sea."*

Ladies, are you motivated to study God's Word to show ourselves approved and to admit when we misrepresent it?

How serious is it to teach our view or the culture's view on any subject matter that contradicts what God's Word says? (Revelation 22:18-19)

We need to take seriously what we are teaching to those younger than us! We will be held accountable by God. We will be going against what the culture is teaching our young women and may face possible persecution. Are you ready for this if you choose to teach younger women?

Did you see anything you have never seen before concerning the teaching of wrong doctrine? What has the Holy Spirit taught you?

Read what Paul said when he came to know and truly understand God's Word. I Timothy 1:13-16 says, *"13 though formerly I was a blasphemer, persecutor, and insolent opponent. But I received mercy because I had acted ignorantly in unbelief, 14 and the grace of our Lord overflowed for me with the faith and love that are in Christ Jesus. 15 The saying is trustworthy and deserving of full acceptance, that Christ Jesus came into the world to save sinners, of whom I am the foremost. 16 But I received mercy for this reason, that in me, as the foremost, Jesus Christ might display his perfect patience as an example to those who were to believe in him for eternal life."*

We all have a former life where we acted in ignorance and unbelief. Jesus came to save the sinner. I am so thankful to have honest people in my life who have encouraged me in my Christian walk, not excused my sin.

Elaine Oostra

LESSON 4
GODLY LIVING

*"Older woman likewise are to be **reverent** in behavior, **not slanderers or slaves to much wine.** They are to teach what is good"* (ESV, Titus 2:3).

Reverent Behavior

Did you know you are a woman of worth? <u>**When you understand how God sees you, you will desire to be more reverent in your behavior**</u>. You won't want to gossip, get drunk, or be promiscuous. You will want to teach what God has shown you about who you are in Him. Teaching those younger than yourself will kept you in check and thinking about your personal behavior and habits. You won't want to fail these young women. You will find yourself continually humbled! I currently lead a Bible study for teen girls and asked them, "What if you found out that I got drunk this past weekend or was gossiping nonstop about everyone?"

"We would not respect you or believe what you taught us," they told me. This comment was the girl's true honesty!

Oh God, keep me reverent in all of my behavior! They are watching me! (And no, I am not in the habit of getting drunk.)

So let's see what God has to say about how He sees us. His Word will show us any behavior that we need to change.

"For I want you to know how great a struggle I have for you and for those at Laodicea and for all who have not seen me face to face, that their hearts may be encouraged, being knit together in love, to reach all the riches of full assurance of understanding and the knowledge of God's mystery, which is Christ, in whom are hidden all the treasures of wisdom and knowledge" (ESV, Colossians 2:1-3).

What do you see about 'you' in these verses?

Yes, Paul has a struggle for you. **What does Paul want for us?**

To be knit _____ in love,

To reach all the riches of _____ _____ of _____ and the _____ of God's mystery which is_____

What two treasures (riches) are not hidden from you, but for us, in Christ?

We have access to wisdom and knowledge when Jesus Christ is our Lord and Savior!

<u>Underline</u> what we are instructed to do when we are in Christ.

"Therefore, as you received Christ Jesus the Lord, so walk in him, rooted and built up in him and established in the faith, just as you were taught, abounding in thanksgiving" (ESV, Colossians 2:6-7).

These are the four instructions you should have underlined.

Walk in Him. Learn how He lived his life on this earth.

Be rooted in Him. In trials, our faith is being tested. Trials develop our faith. It's like manure (fertilizer) around the trees; it helps them grow and have strong, deep roots. If a tree could talk, would it say, "Why are you putting that awful, smelly, gross stuff on me?" The gardener reassures the tree it will help it grow into a strong tall tree. A strong windstorm comes along and the tree, with its roots firmly holding it in place, does not topple over. In our lives, we will have trials. James chapter one tells us. The trials will produce steadfastness (like a tree). We are being perfected, so we will lack in nothing.

Be built up in Him. We need to know who we are in Christ. We need to know our confidence and security is found only in Him. He is our strength. Learn who God says you are. (Re-read lesson one and two.)

Be established in your faith. Study the Word by yourself and with others.

Which one are you struggling with the most in your life? Share how this verse has encouraged you.

"9 For in Him the whole fullness of deity dwells bodily, 10 and YOU have been filled in him, who is the head of all rule and authority … 12 Having been buried with him in baptism in which you were also raised with him through faith in the powerful working of God who raised him from the dead. 13 And you, who were dead in your trespasses and the uncircumcision of your flesh, God made alive together with him, having forgiven us ALL our trespasses" (ESV, Colossians 2: 9-10, 12-13).

How did Christ Jesus give us worth?

We are _____ in Him (vs 10)

Having been _____ with Him in baptism in which you were _____ _____ with Him……(vs 12)

And you, who were _____ (past tense) in your trespasses …….(vs 13)

God made _____ together with Him, having _____ us ALL our trespasses." (vs 13) (Don't pull the old nature off the cross and drag it behind you; it's a rotten dead corpse!)

We did nothing to earn this forgiveness; we are alive because of God!

"But God, being rich in mercy, because of the great love with which he loved us, even when we were dead in our trespasses, made us alive together with Christ - by grace you have been saved- and raised us up with him and seated us with him in the heavenly places in Christ Jesus" (ESV, Ephesians 2:4 -6).

When did God love you?

Where are you seated and *in whom*?

Who saved you?

"For by grace you have been (perfect tense) saved through faith. And this is not your own doing; it is the gift of God, not a result of works, so that no one may boast" (ESV, Ephesians 2:8-9).

Why can't we save ourselves?

Write out John 10:28. Who gave you eternal life? Who has you in His hand? How secure are you in His hand?

According to I Peter 1:5, what will God do for you in His mighty power?

This salvation is past, present and future. You were saved, you are being saved, and you will be saved until you receive this *"salvation ready to be revealed in the last time."*

Do we truly take all this to heart? Why do we turn to other 'things' to find our worth? Do we think what Christ did for us is not enough?

When we don't find our worth in what Christ did for us, we can't give it to the next generation. True or False?

> "Reverence" To show respect or fear. The root idea of the former is "fear." It is used to express the attitude toward God Himself

Can you see that when you know your worth in Christ, this spurs you to want to live for Him, live to glorify Him and not glorify ourselves through gossiping, which tears others down. If we don't understand who we are in Christ, we won't have the urge to live godly, reverent lives. **Do you agree or disagree? Why or why not? Share with the group.**

Let me give you an example I just experienced.

At a Christmas program, I heard the "Hallelujah" song by my grandson's middle school choir. Half way through the song, two high school girls sitting in the front aimlessly tried to get the audience to stand up. A few did, including me. I stood because it felt like I was in the presence of our Holy God! I did not know the historical reason why people stood during this song until now. I learned Handle wrote the song in 1721 and during the time of monarchy in England, rumor had it King George ll stood when he heard the words King of Kings and Lord of Lords. The tradition became when a monarch stood, the common people had to stand out of respect. It was said King George was standing for the greatest monarch, the King of Kings.

You and I live in the presence of the KING daily! Our hearts ought to always have deep respect. It should show in our attitude and actions. Would I gossip if Jesus was standing beside me? No! Would I yell at my husband? No. Perhaps as older women, we are told to be reverent because we are more verbal, and not always careful in what we say. Have we earned the right, as older women, to say what we want? If anything, we are to be even more reverent in our behavior and words.

When we have a reverent respect for God, we will have a reverent respect for others around us. The reverse is true also. If we don't have reverence for God, we will not have reverence for others. We will put others down, become slanderers, making others seem lesser than ourselves.. If we indulge (becoming slaves to much wine) in what makes us happy, life becomes all about "me." Self-centeredness is what makes women feel free to put others down.

When someone messes up or is forgetful, do you get frustrated? Do you let the person know how frustrated you are? Do you let others around you know how this person messed up? I don't know about you, but going through menopause has made me forgetful! Everyone keeps telling me it is part of the process of getting older. Well, I don't like it! What I would like is understanding when I do forget. Maybe even an arm around me, telling me it's okay and that it's not the end of the world. I have been on the receiving end of getting a rebuttal for forgetting. What this person didn't know was I already had given myself 50 lashes! I don't want to be that kind of woman. But I know I have thoughts of frustration. So I am guilty. I want to extend grace as God has extended grace to me. (There is a difference between constructive criticism done in love and just plain critical criticism, done in frustration.)

When we are at the receiving end of someone's frustration, let's learn how not to behave toward others who mess up. We need to have reverence and respect for others. How we treat others reveals how we see God.

When we know who we are in Christ, we learn an awesome respect and reverence for how holy God is! We want to become holy as He is holy. (This will be covered more in a later chapter.)

Elaine Oostra

LESSON 5
RENOUNCE UNGODLINESS

*"For the grace of God has appeared, bringing salvation for all people, training us to **renounce ungodliness** and worldly passions, and **to live self-controlled, upright, and godly lives in the present age**"* (ESV, Titus 2:11-12).

In Daniel, you will see what you are to do when you feel the conviction of the Holy Spirit in your lives. As older women, we need to look at our lives to see if we recognize any false teaching we have believed or where we have rebelled against God in our behavior. Before we go on, take some time to go before your Father in Heaven and ask Him to examine your heart.

In reading the following passage, I want you to have a highlighter or pen. Every time you see the phrases **we have sinned, we have not listened, we have rebelled, we have not obeyed, and we have done wickedly,** circle or highlight them. When you see the words <u>**us, our**</u> and <u>**we,**</u> underline them.

Daniel's Prayer for His People

Daniel 9: 2-15

"2 in the first year of his reign, I, Daniel, perceived in the books the number of years that, according to the word of the LORD to Jeremiah the prophet, must pass before the end of

the desolations of Jerusalem, namely, seventy years. 3 Then I turned my face to the Lord God, seeking Him by prayer and pleas for mercy with fasting and sackcloth and ashes. 4 I prayed to the LORD my God and made confession, saying, "O Lord, the great and awesome God, who keeps covenant and steadfast love with those who love Him and keep His commandments, 5 we have sinned and done wrong and acted wickedly and rebelled, turning aside from your commandments and rules. 6 We have not listened to your servants the prophets, who spoke in your name to our kings, our princes, and our fathers, and to all the people of the land. 7 To you, O Lord, belongs righteousness, but to us open shame, as at this day, to the men of Judah, to the inhabitants of Jerusalem, and to all Israel, those who are near and those who are far away, in all the lands to which you have driven them, because of the treachery that they have committed against you. 8 To us, O LORD, belongs open shame, to our kings, to our princes, and to our fathers, because we have sinned against you. 9 To the Lord our, God belong mercy and forgiveness, for we have rebelled against Him 10 and have not obeyed the voice of the LORD God by walking in His laws, which He set before us by His servants the prophets. 11 All Israel has transgressed your law and turned aside, refusing to obey your voice. And the curse and oath that are written in the Law of Moses the servant of God have been poured out upon us because we have sinned against Him. 12 He has confirmed his words, which He spoke against us and against our rulers who ruled us, by bringing upon us a great calamity. For under the whole heaven there has not been done anything like what has been done against Jerusalem. 13 As it is written in the Law of Moses, all this calamity has come upon us; yet we have not entreated the favor of the LORD our God, turning from our iniquities and gaining insight by your truth. 14 Therefore the LORD has kept ready the calamity and has brought it upon us, for the LORD our God is righteous in all the works that He has done, and we have not obeyed His voice. 15 And now, O Lord our God, who brought your people out of the land of Egypt with a mighty hand, and have made a name for yourself, as at this day, we have sinned, we have done wickedly."

What did Daniel acknowledge? Did you notice that he included himself in what they had been doing wrong? (To me, he was a pretty righteous guy!)

When praying for our nation, have you ever thought of confessing yourself as part of the sin in our nation? Can you say, "We have sinned"?

If **we** can't acknowledge sin in our lives, sadly nothing will change in us. Please don't evaluate yourself, (meaning through your own mindset), but instead, use God's Word. We can't see our own sin sometimes, even when it slaps us in the face.

"Search me, O God, and know my heart! Try me and know my thoughts! And see if there be any grievous way in me, and lead me in the way everlasting!" (ESV, Psalm 139:23-24).

Let's continue with Daniel 9.

¹⁶ "O Lord, according to all your righteous acts, let your anger and your wrath turn away from your city Jerusalem, your holy hill, because for our sins, and for the iniquities of our fathers, Jerusalem and your people have become a byword among all who are around us. ¹⁷ Now therefore, O our God, listen to the prayer of your servant and to his pleas for mercy, and for your own sake, O Lord, make your face to shine upon your sanctuary, which is desolate. ¹⁸ O my God, incline your ear and hear. Open your eyes and see our desolations, and the city that is called by your name. For we do not present our pleas before you because of our righteousness, but because of your great mercy. ¹⁹ O Lord, hear; O Lord, forgive. O Lord, pay attention and act. Delay not, for your own sake, O my God, because your city and your people are called by your name" (Daniel 9: 16-19).

In verse 16-19, what is Daniel's plea?

Did Daniel come before God in his own righteousness? If not, then how?

This, ladies, is how we need to come before God: not in our righteousness but because of God's great mercy and forgiveness. It is then that we learn how to live godly lives. It's ongoing. You and I are being sanctified (being made holy). We need to be like Daniel: continually crying out to God!

LESSON 6
MEANING OF LOVE – STORGE – EROS

*"They are to teach what is good, and so train the young women to **love**....."* (Titus 2:3b-4).

In this next sentence in Titus, we are told to teach what is good and so train others to love. Why? As women, God has given us a desire to be loved, where men feel the need to be respected. (NIV, Ephesian 5:33) *However, each of you also must **love his wife** as he loves himself, and the **wife must respect** her husband.* When we get into studying Titus 2:5, we will learn more in Lesson 12 about this need of respect.

We tend to throw around the word love without even thinking. I love my cat, I love food, and I love it when it rains. I love my spouse. I love my kids. I love my best friend. Did you know each of these types of love has a different meaning? As a mature woman, do we need to know these meanings of love? Yes! So many young women and young girls think they are in love when it may be just an infatuation.

Sin is overlooked and replaced with the phrase, "They are in love, how can it be wrong?" This is heard this a lot from teen girls. They grow up into young women with the same train of thought. They let their feelings lead them into relationships that are sometimes destructive. "Let your heart lead you" or "Go where your heart leads you" are very famous sayings. My own heart gets me into real trouble at times! It requires continual praying, "God create in me a clean heart!" I am going to follow God's Word. The Word of God gives much better instructions on how to live my life than my heart does.

We are going to study the meaning of the word 'love' and what God's Word has to say about it, not our hearts.

There are four Greek words for love: storge, eros, phileo, and agape. We will look at how the meaning of love gets distorted. The first word we will look at is Storge.

STORGE
God created us to have a natural affection, an obligation to treat others kindly.

What are the action words that describe this love in Romans 12:9-10?

"Natural affection is feeling for a wife, husband, child, and sibling. The abiding feeling within a man, ("man" meaning male or female) that rests on something close to him, and he feels good about inside himself. This kind of love is not passionate or erotic; it's a familiar love."

When this kind of love is perverted or lost, what happens to humans in Romans 1:28-32 and II Timothy 3:3?

Opposite of Storge in Greek is Astorgos which means "without love, devoid of affection, without affection to kindred, hard-hearted, unfeeling." What examples can you think of for Astorgos which you see in the world today? Is it because there is a void in the heart of man?

EROS

I am going to take more time and study on this word. There is a lot of confusion on this meaning of love. The definition of eros is portrayed in the Old Testament book, Song of Solomon.

> "**EROS** described the healthy, common expressions of physical love. In the Scriptures, eros primarily refers to those expressions of love carried out between a husband and wife." (Sam O'Neal)

"Eros is the Greek term that describes romantic or sexual love. The term also portrays the idea of passion and intensity of feeling. The word was originally connected with the goddess, Eros, of Greek Mythology.

The meaning of eros is slightly different than our modern term "erotic" because we often associate "erotic" with ideas or practices that are naughty or inappropriate. This wasn't the case with eros. Instead, eros described the healthy, common expressions of physical love. In the Scriptures, eros primarily refers to those expressions of love carried out between a husband and wife."

This word is not used in the New Testament. Eros is the physical, sensual intimacy between a husband and wife. Eros is a word to express sexual love or feeling of arousal between two people. God created sexual intimacy for marriage. Let's look at what the Word teaches us on how to handle the physical feelings outside of marriage.

This type of love needs proper boundaries. What are they in I Corinthians 7:8-9?

Hebrews 13:4

I Corinthians 7:5

"Eros love is part of God's design, a gift of his goodness for procreation and enjoyment. Sex, as God intended it, is a source of delight and a beautiful blessing between a man and a woman who are married to each other." (Sam O'Neal)

How does Proverbs 5:18-19 support this?

"Sexual love is not inherently unclean or evil. Rather, it is the gift of God to married couples to express their love for one another, strengthen the bond between them, and ensure the survival of the human race. The Bible devotes one whole book to the blessings of erotic, or sexual, love—Song of Solomon. The love between a husband and a wife should be, among other things, an erotic love. However, a long-term relationship based solely on eros is doomed to failure. The "thrill" of sexual love wears off quickly unless there are some philia and agapé to go along with it.

"Even though there is nothing inherently sinful with erotic love, it is in this sphere that our sinful nature is easily made manifest because eros focuses primarily on sensuality and self. Storge, philia, and agapé focus on relationship and others. Consider what the apostle Paul tells the Colossian church: *"Put to death therefore what is earthly in you: sexual immorality, impurity, passion, evil desire, and covetousness, which is idolatry"* (Colossians 3:5). The Greek word for "sexual immorality" is porneia (the root of our word, pornography). This essentially covers the gamut of sexual sin (adultery, fornication, homosexuality, bestiality, etc.).

"When shared between husband and wife, erotic love can be a wonderful thing, but because of our fallen sin nature, expressions of eros too often becomes porneia. In dealing with eros, human beings tend to go to extremes, becoming either ascetics (*shunner*) or hedonists (*pleasure seeking*). The ascetic completely avoids sensual or sexual love. The hedonist sees unrestrained sexual passion and all forms of sensuality as perfectly natural and to be indulged. The biblical view is a balance between these two sinful extremes. Within the bond of heterosexual marriage, God celebrates the beauty of sexual love: *"Let my lover come into his garden and taste its choice fruits. I have come into my garden, my sister, my bride; I have gathered my myrrh with my spice. I have eaten my honeycomb and my honey; I have drunk my wine and my milk. Eat, O friends, and drink; drink your fill, O lovers"* (Song of Solomon 4:16—5:1). Outside of biblical marriage, eros becomes distorted and sinful." https://www.gotquestions.org/eros-love.html

We looked up verses on the boundaries of eros love. God loves us so much! He created our bodies, and He knows how they work more than we do. He knows what will happen to us if we have eros outside of His boundaries. We see it, but somehow we ignore the consequences of it and continue to call it 'love.' Please hear me out on this. I want to save lives!

When a man and woman wait until they get married to have sex, save themselves sexually for each other, there is no worry of sexually transmitted diseases. True agape love is always looking out for your loved one. You also don't die from this kind of sex. Remember this.

When we have erotic (eros) sex outside the boundaries of marriage, we are always looking for our pleasure. We take great risk in passing diseases to another person, because our pleasure comes first. Teens learn in school that when you have multiple partners, you are at a risk of getting a sexually transmitted disease. People I know personally have shared with me that they contracted a disease due to unbridled passion outside of marriage and now have to fight it the rest of their lives. They also had to share this with the person they were going to marry.

What does Romans 1:27 tell us about what happens when we believe we can go outside the boundaries of God's Word and then encourage others to do the same?

Why, as a Christian, would we want others to receive a due penalty? Roman 1: 32 tells us it's the death penalty. Doesn't this make your heart sob?

Read Romans 1:24-32 in full context. Why are some of us, as Christians, sending others to their death?

Why do some think it's love to encourage sexual behavior outside of marriage, when they know it is not part of God's plan?

Are there any Scriptures that support a sexual relationship that is not just between a married man and woman?

Is man wiser than God on how He created our bodies to function?

Can we choose to ignore what God's Word says and instead listen to someone else's interpretation of the Scriptures on what God has said?

How do we define what sin is and is not?

We are not beyond falling for Satan's lies! Eve did, and she lived in a sinless world!

Read II Corinthians 11:2-4. How can our pure devotion to Christ be led astray when we receive another gospel (teaching) contrary to what God's Word says?

These are questions we seriously need to ask ourselves when we start to fall into the ways of the world. Please remember I didn't write the Bible, God did. They are His words, not mine. The world is calling the words of God "hate speech." I don't hate; I want others to have life and to have it abundantly! I do not want to send others to death. I will not!

According to I Corinthian 6:9-10, who will not inherit the Kingdom of God? This verse mentions nine categories.

If I do any of these nine things, or someone I care deeply about does, can I change what God's Word has to say about it to please myself or them?

I pray you keep on continuing! Don't give up! Let the Holy Spirit teach you through studying God's Word. Our enemy, Satan, hates it when we realize we had believed the world's way of thinking over what God says. God's Word is like a big search light, showing us the truth. We can choose to shut it off and stay with what we believe to be the truth or look at what God is revealing to us.

Keep on keeping on!

LESSON 7
SUCH WERE SOME OF YOU

*"They are to teach what is good, and so train the young women to **love**....."* (Titus 2:3b-4).

God promises to forgive, even at the last minute of life. We are responsible for telling the truth of God's Word now, even if you share what the Bible says and it is not received or even if you end up in jail accused of hate speech. Is it hate or cowardliness that silences us from speaking the truth?

If my child sins sexually and goes against God's Word, I cannot make their sin acceptable for me to feel better about their eternal destination. I would, for sure, be condemning my child to hell. I have heard people say, "I can never serve a God who would send my loved one to hell." God didn't do it! They had the free choice to obey God's Word or not. If someone we know and love dearly commits adultery, or murders, or steals, we cannot pass a law to make it okay and right in God's sight. Why would we keep God's forgiving love and grace from those we love? I am saddened by Christians who feel that in order to show love, they need to compromise their convictions on what God's Word clearly teaches. We don't. We must not. But, we must have the compassion as Christ had.

I can hear the question, "Why pick on this sin! What about other sins?" First,

ALL sin is against God.

Write out:

Romans 3:23

Psalm 51:4

Matthew 7:2-5

What is Jesus assuming is in our eye?

"The seed of every sin is in every heart." *(Quote by John Owen)*

When we recognize our brokenness with deep humility, any personal righteousness about our sin should embarrass and anger us. We have a commonality with all kinds of sinners. When I teach on sexual sins in my neighbor's eye, I need to see it through the log of my depravity. I need to be more angered by my sin than what sin is in someone else's heart. My heart needs to overflow at how God has forgiven me. But if I am so focused on other people's sin, I am out of touch with the gospel. We cannot push away people who are being deceived about their sexual lifestyle or any sin. Nor can we say, "Peace, peace, all is well!" We all need to be broken and repent. We all need to be born again. Refusing to acknowledge our brokenness keeps us outside of God's grace.

Go back and review I Corinthians 6:9-10.

Please don't let pride keep you from what the Holy Spirit is teaching you from God's Word.

🐇 I understand that those who do not believe in God or have Jesus Christ as their personal Lord and Savior will not believe or apply to their lives what God's Word says. I understand why they would see what I am saying as nonsense and phobic. BUT what I don't get and what makes me weep are those who profess to know the Word of God and condone the behavior that defiles a person. 🐇

As mature women, we need to speak the truth in love. We tend to speak from emotions. We need to teach in love. We need to ask God to show us how. God loved us while we were so messed up. The grace and love He gave to us, we need to give to others.

God never justifies our sin. He disciplines us as His child when we sin because He loves us. My heart's cry is to be holy as He is holy. We are to strive for holiness, not because we have to, but because we want our life to please Him. He sent His Son to die for us!

Write out I Peter 1:15-16.

How are we to be holy?

Read Romans 12:1-2. What are our bodies to be? How are we transformed? What is the will of God?

When people say they were born a certain way, so it's not their fault if their desires are against what God's Word says, I tell them I too was born this way. I was born with a sin nature, just like every single person born since the beginning of time, because of Adam and Eve sinning (Jeremiah 17:9, the heart is deceitfully wicked). Each of us may struggle with different temptations. What tempts me may not tempt you. What tempts you, I may not struggle with, BUT we ALL have weaknesses. Jesus came to die for all our sins and temptations! If He hadn't, we all would be doomed!

🐇 According to the American Psychiatric Associates, "the causes of sexual orientation (whether homosexual or heterosexual) are not known at this time, and likely are multifactorial including biological and behavioral roots which may vary between different individuals and may even vary over time. No findings have emerged that permit scientists to conclude that sexual orientation is determined by any particular factor or factors."

Kevin DeYoung wrote a book called, *What Does the Bible Really Teach about*

Homosexuality? I highly recommend this book if you would like more information on this subject. 🐇

"And *such were some of you. But you were* **washed***, you were* **sanctified***, you were* **justified** *in the name of the Lord Jesus Christ and by the Spirit of our God"* (ESV, I Corinthians 6:11).

This is a powerful verse! **And such <u>were</u> some of you**. Our culture and, sadly, some of our churches are keeping others from being washed, sanctified and justified. The truth of God's Word has been exchanged for a lie. My heart cries for those who will not inherit eternal life. My heart trembles in fear for those who condone what God calls sin. Lord Jesus, please forgive us! Does your heart cry and tremble in fear for these people?

Our pride does not want us to believe that we could be deceived. No matter how we try and justify what God calls sin, it doesn't change what God's Word says! Did you ever read in the Old Testament what happens to people who changed God's Word to fit their lifestyle? It did not end well for them!

Adam and Eve had perfect fellowship with God, but they fell prey to Satan's tactics, (Genesis 3). They took their eyes off of God and fixated them on the forbidden fruit. None of us are beyond being deceived.

What forbidden fruit is Satan handing to us that we may be giving to others and tempting them to sin? Be honest!

Are we so focused on the sin of others that we do not even see our own?

Twenty years ago I never thought I would need to write a Bible study regarding God ordaining marriage for a man and a woman. I innocently believed if you were a Christian, you understood and knew why God created sex and for whom. You also knew that God's Word was the same yesterday, today and tomorrow. Today many Christians seem to be looking at society rather than God's Word. Could it be because our belief in God's Word is being challenged legally and there truly is a cost to following Jesus Christ?

"Got Questions: "Can/Should we interpret the Bible as literal?"

Answer: Not only can we take the Bible literally, but we must take the Bible literally. This is the only way to determine what God really is trying to communicate to us. When we read any piece of literature, but especially the Bible, we must determine what the author intended to communicate. Many today will read a verse or passage of Scripture and then give their own definitions to the words, phrases, or paragraphs, ignoring the context and authors' intent. But this is not what God intended, which is why God tells us to correctly handle the Word of truth (II Timothy 2:15).

Finally, when we make ourselves the final arbiters of which parts of the Bible are to be interpreted literally, we elevate ourselves above God. Who is to say, then, that one person's interpretation of a biblical event or truth is more or less valued than another's? The confusions and distortions that would inevitably result from such a system would essentially render the Scriptures null and void. The Bible is God's Word to us and He meant it to be believed. Literally and completely."

I take so seriously what I teach these impressionable, young girls and am very cautious. God forbid I hand them a forbidden fruit. I know I will be held accountable! I am seeing and hearing more boldness of the world's point of view from youth. "Well they are in love, how can it be wrong?" Some youth believe sex before marriage with whomever, living together, and sexual relations between the same sexes are fine. Satan's biggest lie to these girls is "it's not hurting anyone". Yet, I witness the devastation in these girls' lives.

My heart cries for teens! Some don't, or can't, connect the unbiblical choices their parent(s) have made to the turmoil they are living. It's too hard for them to face the truth of a parent(s) life choices. I can understand how difficult that would be. You have to be so gentle when you talk to them. Be sure to never put down their parent(s). Just gently tell them to believe God's Word. Otherwise you are wasting your time having Bible studies with them. Share with them that His Word is to teach us to have the life He meant for us to have and have it abundantly. Only God can open a person's eyes to see the truth of His Word. We are called to teach God's Word. But, we can't make someone receive it.

Elaine Oostra

LESSON 8
MEANING OF LOVE - PHILEO – AGAPE

*"They are to teach what is good, and so train the young women to **love**"* (Titus 2:3b-4).

Definition Phileo

φιλέω **philéō,** fil-eh'-o; to be a friend to (fond of (an individual or an object)), i.e. have affection for (denoting personal attachment, as a matter of sentiment or feeling; embracing especially the judgment and the deliberate assent of the will as a matter of principle, duty and propriety; specially, to kiss (as a mark of tenderness):—kiss, love.

PHILEO

Phileo is a companionable love, rich in emotion, brotherly love, a friendship-type love and non-sexual. It's not a love toward our enemies. It is warmth and affection toward another person. I think of this love when I watch my grandkids do or say something that warms my heart.

We don't have this toward someone who treats us badly or hurts us. When we learn agape love, we may experience phileo toward difficult people. At times, this love can be shallow and conditional. It can depend on how others treat us.

I Thessalonians 4:9

I Samuel 18:1-3

Romans 12:10

Hebrews 13:1

According to Jude 1, what name does Jude have for those who are called?

Phileo is the love we have for fellow believers. Phileo love involves giving as well as receiving. This love is higher than eros love because it's **our** happiness rather than **my** happiness. This love is called out of one's heart by qualities in another. BUT this love can fail when significantly strained; it can collapse in a crisis. This love is still conditional and natural.

AGAPE

Agape Love

(noun) selfless love of one person for another without sexual implications (especially love that is spiritual in nature)

Agape love involves faithfulness, commitment, and an act of the will. It is distinguished from the other types of love by its lofty moral nature and strong character. Agape love is beautifully described in I Corinthians 13.

Agape is the love God commands us to have toward each other. It includes those who hurt us, are rude to us, hate us, and people we clash with as far as personalities. It also includes those who persecute us because of our faith.

Read Matthew 5:44

Some contrasts between agape and phileo are as follows:

Phileo	Agape
Natural	Learned
Emotional	Volitional
Discriminatory	Non-discriminatory
Conditional	Unconditional
Pleasure	Preciousness
Delight	Esteem
Liking	Prizing
Because of	In spite of
Fails	Never fails

Agape can't be earned. It delights in giving. It keeps on loving when the loved one is unresponsive, unkind, unlovable, and unworthy. It's unconditional. It is a consuming passion for the well-being of others. It would do nothing to jeopardize the other person.

John 3:16

Agape love is beautifully described in I Corinthians 13. Write down what love IS -

IS NOT –

We can only agape love others when we see them through God's eyes. This love has nothing to do with feelings, unlike the other meanings of love. Agape is a will of the mind. It is obedience to God. It's an action word.

What is agape love? Write out the following Scriptures.

John 17:26

Romans 5:5, 8

Galatians 5:22

In John 13:35 and I John 3:16, what does this love look like for us?

Summarize what you learned about the word 'love'. How can you use this teaching for younger women?

What kind of love should we have toward our spouse? Toward our children? Family? Friends?

How has the study of the word 'love' helped you understand more of God's love for you?

Do you see how God's love is unconditional and our love is conditional?

Lord Jesus, help us to love one another as you love us! Help us to see others through Your eyes and how much You love us all, no more no less! We are all made in the image of God. Help us to tell Your truths and help us not to cast others off as hopeless. You loved the woman caught in adultery. While others condemned her, You were an advocate for her. You forgave her and told her to go sin no more. It was the same with the woman at the well. The disciples couldn't believe You would even talk to someone like her, but you saw her worth! Many believed because of her testimony. Help us to love as You love!

LESSON 9
PATTERN FOR MARRIAGE

*"They are to teach what is good, and so train the young women to **love**....."* (Titus 2:3b-4).

Let's go back to Genesis 2:21-25 and look at the first wedding. It's not like today. Adam and Eve didn't have to get a marriage license or send out an invitation. There was no one to invite! We have pastors or judges officiate our weddings; Adam and Eve had God. God is the inventor of marriage, not man.

Read Genesis 2:18-25.

What is the first thing God said about the man?

All the animals had mates, but no mate was found for Adam. Verse 20 says, *"there was not found a **helper** fit for him."*

> **helper** (Hb. 'ezer) is one who supplies strength in the area that is lacking in "the helped." This term does not imply that the helper is either stronger or weaker than the one helped. *(cf ESV footnote)*

God puts Adam to sleep. What does God take out of the man?

Who was fashioned from the rib?

Go back to Genesis 2:7. How did God make Adam?

🐰 Because I love this passage in Genesis, I am going to go down a short trail. I want you to know this for yourself and to be able to teach it. God has His hands on us! He breathes life into us! We have no right to take it from any person, in or out of the womb.

What did God breathe into Adam? (This breath is spiritual, mental, and physical into the one to bear His image!) **Read and write out Job 33:4.**

How did God create animals, fish, and birds?

What did God use to create man and woman? Imagine a potter fashioning clay.

Physical Breath

Is God still forming us today and breathing life into us? (Psalm 139:13-14)

Spiritual Breath

"That which is born of the flesh is flesh, and that which is born of the Spirit is spirit. Do not marvel that I said to you, 'You must be born again.' The wind blows where it wishes, and you hear its sound, but you do not know where it comes from or where it goes. So it is with everyone who is born of the Spirit." (ESV, John 3:6-8).

How is spiritual breath different than physical breath?

I hope you enjoyed that little trail! Back to Adam and Eve and marriage!

It was important for you to look up how Adam was created versus how God made Eve. It has to do with the covenant of marriage. We are going to study this shortly. Just hang in there with me as we go through this passage on the first wedding.

In Genesis 2:23, Adam is awake. What does he say?

The first wedding was in a beautiful garden! (And man thinks he invented outdoor weddings.)

In Genesis 2:24, how is the standard of all future marriages defined?

In Matthew 19:4-6, how did God make Adam and Eve? What shall the two become? What are they not?

This, ladies, is the pattern for marriage which we are to teach. I think it's exciting! God established this pattern in the Old Testament and reaffirmed it in the New Testament. His plans for a man and a woman to become one flesh has not changed!

🐰 Here is something to think about. Did God give Adam more than one wife? Did God give Adam another man? We already know the animals were not suitable for Adam. But sadly, man tries to change God's pattern and twist Scripture to his way of thinking. What God ordained from the beginning of time is set in stone. There are no Scriptures that change the meaning of marriage of one man to one woman. None.

In Romans 8:7, why is the world changing what God has ordained for marriage?

We need to ask ourselves if we have a mind that is hostile toward God. Have you, like me, ever thought that way when you want to do it your way? Oh Lord forgive us when we do! 🐰

Strongs Concordance

ishshah – woman, wife, female

Original Word: נָשִׁים
Part of Speech: Noun Feminine
Transliteration: ishshah
Phonetic Spelling: (ish-shaw')
Short Definition: wife

The Hebrew word for "wife" is gender- specific and means woman.

The Bible in Genesis shows us that Eve came from Adam's side. She was flesh of his flesh. The two became *one flesh.* God was showing us the essential of marriage and that it's meant to be forever, till death do us part. Divorce is so painful because it is tearing away this *one flesh.*

When I teach this lesson to teen girls, I take two pieces of paper and glue them together to make a visual picture of *one flesh*. I then try to pull the pieces of paper apart, and it's a torn mess. Each piece, even though torn, has pieces of the other paper stuck to it. Why? The *one flesh* means glued, stuck together for eternity. No man can separate it. Remember, till death do us part.

Marriage is the commitment we make, a covenant before God. I then ask the girls of divorced parents if they could have their biological parents together, would they? They ALL say, "Yes!" I explain to them that this is why God hates (yet permits under certain circumstances) divorce; it hurts the kids and families, shredding them like the paper I tore. It causes so much pain. I hear parents say, "Oh, the kids will be fine. They will get over it." No, they won't. Women in their 60s still hurt from their parents' divorce. I understand in a marriage where there is infidelity or abuse, it would be painful to stay married. Biblically you can leave. Your safety and your children come first. I am just telling you the deep yearning I hear from teens that just want their first parents back together! I remind them we live in a sin-filled world and there are no perfect families out there.

I want us, as mature Christian women, to teach the younger how to find a godly mate, to learn to wait and not to settle for whatever is out there. I want them to know who they are in Christ first and the guy they are dating to know who he is in Christ first. Maybe this will cut down the divorce rate among Christians.

As mature women, we need to be teaching these young women what to look for in a mate. They need to know how to see warning signs. If girls are sexually active before marriage, they will become blind and ignore all the flashing neon lights that are blaring at them! Their minds tell them it will get better once they are married. Those of us who are married know that is the biggest lie we can tell ourselves. What you see is what you get! Past behavior predicts future behavior UNLESS God gets a hold of their hearts, and they submit their lives to Him. Until then, DON'T marry the guy! I am also talking to the women who are no longer teenagers and looking to remarry or be married for the first time.

LESSON 10
MARRIAGE AS A COVENANT

*"And so train the young women **to love their husbands and children**"* (ESV, Titus 2:4).

What is a covenant?

In Lesson 6, we looked at God's pattern for marriage in light of the meanings of the definitions of love. Now we are going be looking deeper into the definition of marriage.

The first mention of marriage being a covenant is found in Malachi 2:14, 15, *"Because the LORD was witness between you and the wife of your youth, to whom you have been faithless, though she is your companion and your wife by **covenant**. Did he not make them one, with a portion of the Spirit in their union? And what was the one God seeking? Godly offspring. So guard yourselves in your spirit, and let none of you be faithless to the wife of your youth."*

What does this passage teach about marriage and children?

COVENANT 1: a usually formal, solemn, and binding agreement: Compact 2. a written agreement or promise usually under seal between two or more parties especially for the performance of some action. https://www.merriam-webster.com/dictionary/covenant
A covenant marriage is intended by God to be a lifelong relationship exemplifying unconditional love, reconciliation, sexual purity, and growth. A covenant is an eternal commitment with God. People can negotiate out of contracts, but not out of a covenant. The heart of covenant marriage is "the steadfast love of the Lord," which comes from the very heart of God and "never ceases" (Lamentations 3:22, Revised Standard Version).

The one kind of covenant that's never broken is when God makes a covenant with us. This is called an **unconditional covenant**. God always keeps His word. All the other covenants are broken that are made from man to man or man to God. These are called **conditional covenants**. Meaning one party does not keep his word or backs out of covenant. If you want to do an in-depth study on covenants, I highly recommend the Bible study *Precept Upon Precept: Covenant* by Kay Author. It's one of my favorite studies!

When a covenant was made in the Bible, there was an exchange of something or a sign (for instance, a rainbow promised by God not to flood the whole earth again). A shoe handed to a person or a **cutting** of something represented a covenant. *(The Hebrew Berith means "a cutting.)* Blood was shed in covenants. There was a mingling of blood. In the Old Covenant, the Israelites had to sacrifice animals for the forgiveness of their sins. Hebrews 10:4 tells us this never took away sin. The Old Covenant was a picture of the New Covenant, Jesus' death on the cross. *"We have been made holy through the sacrifice of the body of Jesus Christ **once for all**"* (New International Version, Hebrews 10:10).

 I really would love for you to do this precept study on covenant!

Marriage is a covenant. There is a shedding of blood when two become one. God created our bodies. He placed in women **a hymen**. Did you ever wonder why?

The hymen [hahy-muh n] noun, Anatomy
a fold of mucous membrane partly closing
the external orifice of the vagina in a virgin.

When a married couple comes together for the first time sexually, the hymen breaks, and there is the shedding of blood, a sign of a covenant. Of course with remarriage, this does not happen, but God is revealing to us how serious He takes marriage and the promise a couple who marries is making. It is a covenant relationship.

Look up Ephesians 5:31. What do man and woman become when they leave their father and their mother?

When God spoke of two people being joined as one, He was referring to something we're only beginning to understand in a real, physiological way. When two people are intimate, the hypothalamus in the brain releases chemicals that induce feelings of attachment and trust. Having sex outside of marriage results in a person forming an attachment and trusting someone with whom he or she does not have a committed relationship. The definition of trust in the mind deteriorates. To have that kind of link with someone without the security of working together toward God is dangerous. Two individuals who are—even mildly—physiologically obsessed with each other, but not committed to growing in God as a couple, can be torn from God and His plans for them.

There are many reasons God ordained marriage. Let's look up some verses. (Some you have already looked up).

Genesis 2:18

Malachi 2:13-16

What is God seeking? (vs. 15)

Why does God want us to be faithful to our spouses? (vs. 16)

What are we protected from in marriage? (I Corinthians 7:2)

What does Proverbs 18:22 say about marriage? (If you have a Message version of the Bible, look it up in there and other versions.)

Marriage is a picture of Christ and His Church.

Read Ephesians 5:25-26 and answer the following questions.

What did Christ do for His bride?

How is this an example of what husbands are to do?

For us as wives, we are not off the hook. What are we to do according to Ephesians 5:22-24?

When will the bride of Christ, the Church (us), be united with Him? (Revelation 19:7-9, 21:1-2 and 22:20)

Can you remain unmarried? (I Corinthians 7:7-9, 32-35,37)

When should you be married? (I Corinthians 7: 1-2)

Do you now have a better understanding of the covenant of marriage? Share what you learned.

LESSON 11
SELF-CONTROL

*"to be **self-controlled**, pure, working at home, kind,"* (English Standard Version, Titus 2:5a).

"Older men are to be sober-minded, dignified, self-controlled" (ESV, Titus 2:2).

Men are called to be self-controlled as women are. It's a fruit of the Spirit!

"But the fruit of the Spirit is love, joy, peace, patience, kindness, goodness, faithfulness, gentlenesses, self-control; against such things there is no law. And those who belong to Christ Jesus have crucified the flesh with its passions and desires. If we live by the Spirit, let us also keep in step with the Spirit. Let us not become conceited, provoking one another, envying one another" (Galatian 5:22-26).

Look up the following verses on self-control.

II Peter 1:5-7

II Timothy 1:7

Proverbs 16:32

Titus 2:11-14

Galatians 5:21-23

James 3:1-18

What things in life cause you to feel out of control?

How do you handle feeling out of control?

🐰 There was a time in my life self-control was a struggle. My need to be in control caused many areas of my life to be out of control. Fear fueled anger. When I got angry, I would yell at my kids. Most Sundays I would leave the house yelling at my husband for not being the spiritual leader then slam the door behind me. It was not pretty. I'm NOT proud of it! My kids wouldn't want to go because Dad didn't have to. Then I would sit in church fuming with four crabby kids beside me. Wow, weren't we a spiritual bunch! I can laugh at it now. I know some of you can visualize this scene.

Do I wish I had handled it much better? Oh, YES! I wish I would have shown my children the joy of fellowshipping with others, regardless of whether my husband came along or not.

I was trying too hard to be the Holy Spirit to my husband. It was not until I finally released him that I had peace. He came to church!

The fuel of fear diminished as I trusted God more. I share more about this in, *"One Brick At a Time."* A story of God's redemption and healing in my life. 🐰

Ok, I was brave enough to share my lack of self-control. It's your turn!

"Do not be conformed to this world, but be transformed by the renewal of your mind, that by testing you may discern what is the will of God, what is good and acceptable and perfect" (ESV, Romans 12:2).

As a woman, how can we have self-control?

How can you renew your mind?

Titus 2:5a says, *"To be self-controlled, pure, working at home, kind,"*

Now we hit the hard part of this verse. I am not going to go too deeply into this. I find it interesting that we are first told to be self-controlled as the men are. Then we are told to be pure. Stuck in the middle of this verse is "working at home." Then we are told to be kind. Odd order, or is it?

Read I Timothy 5:13. What five things have these women learned to do? Should they be doing these things?

Why should they not be doing these things? Read Titus 2 the last part of verse 5. What were they doing to the Word of God?

Why do you think working at home is put in the middle? This is just something to think about.

When we get older and our children leave home, we realize how fast time went. It's time you never get back with your kids. Our kids are in our lives forever, hopefully! A job is not. A job will not come and visit you when you are old. Finding the balance between work and kids is difficult. Something or someone, suffers. We delude ourselves into thinking otherwise. There is only so much time in a day; eight to nine hours is taken up by a job and kids maybe get four to five hours of their parents' time each day. Time is what they want, not things. I am not bashing working parents. I worked when my kids were all in school. But I saw how easily my work consumed me. I got praised for the great job I did. That never happens at home! IF there is any way you can be home raising your children when they are babies to five years old, please do! No one can love them and teach them how to be the human beings you want them to be like you can. There is a security only you can build in them. So many opportunities to teach them about the Lord throughout your day are missed. I know when I came home from work, I was tired.

You don't have to agree with me. I know there are moms who would love to stay home. I want to encourage you to find the best balance for family and work.

Proverbs 31 is the well-known passage about the wife and mother of excellence. From the description of her, we learn that this mother did work outside of the home. However, her family never lacked anything. She maintained a proper balance, so her family never suffered. Her family was always her priority. While the Bible leaves women the choice as to whether to stay at home with the children or go to work outside the home, it certainly is a commendable thing for a mother to be at home with the children and devote herself to training them full time. Women are encouraged in Titus 2, I Timothy 5, and Deuteronomy 11:19 to stay at home with their young children. Whatever a woman chooses, she must maintain her home as a priority and her primary sphere of influence.

Recommended Resource: *Discovering the Treasures of a Godly Woman: Proverbs 31* by Elizabeth George. I highly recommend Elizabeth George's book if you want to do a deeper study.

Elaine Oostra

LESSON 12
SUBMISSION

*"and **submissive** to their own husbands"* (ESV, Titus 2:5b).

*"Then the L*ORD* God said, 'It is not good that the man should be alone; I will make him a helper fit for him.' Now out of the ground the L*ORD* God had formed every beast of the field and every bird of the heavens and brought them to the man to see what he would call them. And whatever the man called every living creature, that was its name. The man gave names to all livestock and to the birds of the heavens and to every beast of the field. But for Adam there was not found a helper fit for him"* (ESV, Genesis 2:18-20).

What is God's purpose for a woman?

In whose image is the woman created?

Are men and women equal in worth?

Do men and women have the same identical role in life? Back up your answer with Scripture.

In Genesis 3:16, to the woman God said….

In Genesis 3:17, to Adam God said…..

Even though we are equal in God's sight, women are more of a nurturer, caring for the young, while men are better equipped to provide for and protect the family. Each has a different role to play in a Christian marriage. God created us this way, but we fight it, especially as women.

Genesis 3:16b *"your desire shall be for your husband, and he will rule over you."* Think about what this verse is saying. We, as a woman want to be loved by our man. But, there is something else we want to do. We will desire to control our husbands. I know women who, shall we say, wear the pants in the family! I have tried! The verse goes on to say, *"he will rule over you."* Does it sound like there would be a conflict in this house? It is the battle of the sexes!

Is there a power struggle in your home?

Does this verse mean a man is to rule over his wife? Read Ephesians 5:25-30. (We will get into this later.)

If you answered "yes", use Scripture to back your answer.

When I was fist married, I looked to my husband to fulfill my every need. (Just like the Bible said, *"your desire shall be for your husband".*) **Who only can meet my deepest needs?**

When you turn to your husband to meet your needs, who are you not turning to? Are we to have other gods? (Exodus 20:3)

If you want your husband to meet all your needs, what kind of power do you give him? Could he use this to rule over you?

Now that you have looked deeper into Genesis 3:16b, do you see how this verse has been misquoted and misunderstood?

🐰 **Ruling was a result of the fall of man. Man ruling over his wife was not God's original intent. Childbirth was not meant to be painful. The desire for substitute gods and all the pain in the world came because of this fall. If we think God's original plan was to have a man rule over his wife, then we have to include pain and brokenness as part of God's original intentions.** 🐰

We are reminded in Titus 2:4 that older (mature) women are to teach the younger women to love their husbands and children. We, as younger women, had to learn how to love our husbands and children. Because of the fall of man, it's not a natural desire in us. We have seen generation after generation of women not wanting to be submissive to their husbands. Many husbands, because of the fall of man, abused this submission because they are not under the submission of Christ.

Are you rebelling to the word submit? I know I did until I learned what it meant. Let's take a rabbit trail and look it up.

Submit = Greek hupotasso. Better translated "to identify with" – "to be in support of"

"It has nothing to do with being subordinate to, secondary to, or subject to. The correct meaning is especially important and clear when considered against the cultural backdrop, that is to say, when it is understood in the light of the marriage customs and the culture of the people Paul was writing to."

Who are we to submit to first? Write out James 4:7.

Who else are we supposed to submit to according to Ephesians 5:21?

According to I Corinthians 11:2-3, what makes it easy for a wife to submit to her husband?

Who did Christ submit to in John 5:30?

Did Christ give up his worth? Do you give up your worth when you submit to your husband?

Some women have believed they needed to submit to every man. Read Ephesians 5:22-24. To whom is she only to submit?

What is submission a picture of in verse 24?

What does I Peter 3:1 say about an unbelieving spouse?

When wives submit to their husbands, to whom are they submitting according to Ephesians 5:22?

To be fair, let's look at the husband's responsibility. Who does I Peter 3:7 say he will give an account to if he is selfish or domineering? He will give an account one day!

In Ephesians 5:25a, 28, 33a, what is a husband commanded to do?

What do we as women long for in marriage?

Women, we are not off the hook! Read Ephesians 5:33b. Write it out.

Why are men commanded to love and why are women commanded to respect? (This changed my attitude as a wife when the Holy Spirit convicted me!)

Men and women are different. We have different needs in a marriage. A man desires respect from his wife. A woman longs to be loved by her man. A wife can deeply wound her husband when she disrespects him as a man. Women who usurp authority (meaning taking control over every decision in the home) over their husbands and take away their leadership in the home are teaching their children unbiblical truths. We will be accountable to God. Also when we tear down our husbands to others, we will answer to God for this disrespect. (Men are not off the hook, but this study is not for them.)

A great book to read is called *Love and Respect* by Emerson Eggerichs. This book helped me to grow a wife in learning to respect my husband. Also a Bible study by Kay Author called *Marriage Without Regrets* was inspiring and biblical grounded teaching on marriage.

These resources are recommended because marriage can be difficult. Paul even warned us. I know some of you will not have an easy man to submit to or respect. I highly recommend these books to give you the tools in your marriage. I pray you will see a change in yourself as well as your husband. My husband changed because I changed first. As women, we create the atmosphere in our homes. You've heard the saying "If mama ain't happy, ain't nobody happy." It's true!

This change is not an overnight change. Read James 1:1-8. God is doing something in you. He did in me!

Elaine Oostra

LESSON 13

HONOR GOD WITH OUR LIVES

*"That the word of God may not be **reviled**"* (ESV, Titus 2:5c).

What does it mean "that the word of God may not be reviled"? Here are some other Bible translations of this verse. The New American Standard Version says, "so that the word of God will not be dishonored". The New International Version says, "so that no one will malign the word of God". The New Living Translation says, "will not bring shame on the word of God". The Common English Bible says, "so that God's word won't be ridiculed". The Easy-to-Read says, "no one will be able to criticize the teaching God gave us".

Look up the following verses to let Scripture interpret Scripture.

II Corinthians 9:13

I Peter 2:12

I Peter 3:15

I Corinthians 1:18

Titus 2: 7-10

Romans 8:7-8

Let's look a little deeper to understand God's calling on us as His people. Why do you think God created you and me?

We are created for God's holiness NOT our happiness. Women, if we focus on our happiness, we are in big trouble!

Colossians 1:16b, "all things were created _____ and _____Him."

According to Ephesians 4:24, in whose likeness are we created?

According to Isaiah 43:7, in whose glory are we created and why?

Did you see anything in these verses about your personal happiness? I hear more women than I care to count say, "I divorced him because I wasn't happy and God wants me happy." Excuse me, but which chapter and verse says it's about your happiness?

What is God's calling on our lives as believers as mentioned in I Peter 1:15-16?

This is a hard verse to comprehend. Later I will explain how we can become holy.

Let us look at why some may struggle with this passage in I Peter. When we have false standards of God's Word, we believe false teachings; we believe we are not required to live holy lives, and then we encourage others not to as well. Our enemy (Satan) creates a theology for believers to doubt. That leads to a perversion of God's Word.

> **"Perversion** means the alteration of something its original course or meaning; a corruption of what was first intended."

We live in a world that is perverting the True Gospel. None of us are smarter than God, yet we can act like we are.

Write out Hebrews 12:14.

This is God's calling on my life and your life as a born again believer in Jesus Christ. If we do not get this understanding in our lives as believers in Jesus Christ, we dishonor God's Word. We believe the culture's way of thinking over God's unchanging Word. Jesus is the same yesterday, today, and tomorrow. We repress what we instinctively know in our conscience. We were born to know right from wrong, BUT we can come to a point where we no longer listen to our conscience. We legitimize wrong by legalizing it. God will let us have our way... for a time, giving us time to repent, because of His love for us!

I am still in the process of learning what it means for us to be holy as God is Holy. God's Word is **inerrantly Holy,** without any error. God is absent of even a trace of sin: His love is Holy, His mercy is Holy, His wrath is Holy, and His anger is Holy. Because of this, NO sin will be in Heaven to attack us! I know to be holy means to be set apart from the world. I know I need to live by God's standards and not the world's.

"For we are his workmanship, created in Christ Jesus for good works, which God prepared beforehand, that we should walk in them"(ESV, Ephesians 2:10).

HOW CAN WE BECOME HOLY?

I can't make myself holy, no matter how hard I try. So how can we become holy? Holiness only results from a right relationship with God by believing Jesus Christ as Savior.

Read John 3:16

Read Hebrews 12:2

We only increase in **practical holiness** (practicing, striving for, pursuing) as we mature spiritually. Pursuing holiness, means we want to die to our sinful nature not encourage it. Before we were saved, we enjoyed our sin. God has set us apart (being made holy) for honorable use. Left on our own and even in a perfect world, being holy would never happen!

HOW DOES GOD WORK HOLINESS IN US?

I want you to write down a difficult situation you are going through in which you are questioning God.

Read Romans 5:3-5. What do our suffering and our trials produce in us?

What has God given to us?

Read I Peter 1:6-7. What are we told to do in trials? Why is our faith tested? What should be found?

Bear with me, I have a point I am getting to!
Read Proverbs 17:3. What does the Lord do with our hearts?

How is God working holiness in us?

God is purifying us of sin. Sin is unholy. Did you ever look at a trial in your life as God making you holy?

I had you write down a difficult situation you are going through. Now, I want you to write the following phrase above what you wrote with a different color of pen: "God is in the process of making me holy!" This is my point! Yay! This helps us to see that God knows and He has a purpose which we cannot yet see.

WHY DO WE WANT TO BECOME HOLY?

According to Titus 2:7-8, what kind of an example do we want to be to others? Why?

Read II Timothy 2:12. What happens if we endure?

In reading James 1:2-4, what does testing of our faith produce? What is the perfect result?

We are made complete, lacking in nothing! Girls, God is making us holy! Trials make us trust God more and trust less in our abilities. It should be less of us and more of Him. God works this holiness in us. Because of our sinful nature, it usually takes trials to work holiness in us.

"Blessed is the man who remains steadfast under trial, for when he has stood the test, he will receive the crown of life, which God has promised to those who love him" **(ESV, James 1:12). What will you receive?**

Summarize what you have learned and how our behavior could bring ridicule, shame, and dishonor and malign God's Word? How does pursuing holiness bring honor to God's Word?

"If we confess our sins, He is faithful and just to forgive us" (ESV, I John 1:9).

Well done, good and faithful women! I have written another study geared toward teens on the same subjects that are in this study. I want to encourage you. Now that you have gone through this Bible study, my hope is that you feel more prepared to teach those younger than you.

Elaine Oostra

ROLE MODELS

What a better way to end this study than to read testimonies of girls and women who had another woman in their life that has made an impact on them. I had fun collecting these letters. Notice when you read how ordinary women that are mentioned by the writer have made an impact. I hope this encouraged you! Teaching the younger women can be done in a Bible study, but mainly it's our lifestyle that needs to reflect Christ. In reading these letters, you will also read what the younger women see in us as the mature women. They are watching us!

Anna E. (Age 20)

Throughout middle school, I didn't really have women in my life that I could go to for help. In high school, that all changed. Everywhere I looked I had role models that I could go to. For example, I had my high school counselor, librarian, and my grandma. Now that I am in college I find myself still using these ladies as role models. I also have made new friends and have found that I can trust one friend in particular.

My high school counselor and librarian have helped me deal with friendship and depression. High school people are not nice to others and being someone who doesn't feel like they fit in just made it that much harder to socialize with others around me. They would give me tips on how to approach people and ask if I could hang out. Being born with a disability, it was hard for me to do school work, let alone hang out with friends. I can still do the same stuff my friends were doing, but I couldn't do everything.

My grandma has helped me learn to love me for who I am. She also taught me how to think differently about life. I tend to focus on the negatives. My grandma would remind me about the simple things in life and use that as positive things in life. My grandma has also shown me what it means to live by faith, not just read it. I see my grandma read her Bible and pray and she has a very positive outlook on life (as far as I can see). She always makes time and room for God and her Bible. I am off and on in this aspect. I know that it's an excuse to say "Oh I'm too busy" or "I don't have time", but as my high school counselor said: "If God laid down His life and took the time for that, then you have time to pray and give Him time." The last quote from high school that has stuck with me is from my librarian. "Prayer doesn't have to be long and thoughtful. It can be short and sweet and still have the same meaning." What I got from that is I don't have to make it a long prayer. It can just be a short little prayer about anything like a test in school or a family issue that is going on.

Sydney Sue (Age 15)

I have always loved Betsey. I have pictures of her holding me as a toddler, and I find that extraordinary that I am still connected to her today. Every time I see her, I can't help but smile. She just has that way about her. I remember the first time I realized how much she loved God.

A few years ago (2013), she got up at our youth church camp and sang an original song. Being only 13 at the time, I wasn't emotional, but the way she closed her eyes and poured her heart and soul into that song made me cry. Flash forward to last year's (2015) church camp where we had altar night. Again, even at 15, I still never was an emotional crier, but that night I started to tear up as everyone around me was crying. Finally, I let the tears shed, and I poured out myself to God, and I gave Him everything: my family, my possessions, my problems, everything.

I made eye contact with Betsey, and I sat by her and told her everything. After patiently listening, she finally said, "You're free, Sydney." She then prayed over me and what was shocking was that I didn't think that it was Betsey that was talking to me, but God. God talked to me that night through Betsey. Through her, it was the first time I felt like I got answers from Him. When we worshiped later that night, she threw her hands up in the air and praised and praised and praised. She showed me that it's okay to give yourself over to Him. It's okay to throw your hands up in the air and praise. It's okay to be yourself.

Betsey has given me so much. She makes me feel loved and wanted. She makes me feel like I'm worth something when I feel low. I can always count on her to listen to all my problems. She made me realize that we are all human and we are all pretty screwed up somehow. Even Betsey has a dark past that brought me to tears, but in that darkness is when we shine the brightest.

She has not only done so much for me, but also for my church. She works there, but I never feel like it's a job for her. She wants to be there. You can always count on Betsey to give you a hug or kiss. That's just who she is. However, my favorite thing about Betsey is that even though it isn't my middle name, she is the only one to call me Sydney Sue. She truly is a blessing. I love you, Betsey!

Joanna C (Age 28)

Wow, I wish I could summarize in one paragraph or two an answer to mentors in my life, but I can't! There have been so many amazing women who have poured into my life, praying over me, speaking into my challenges, and setting honest examples for me.

I think of my youth leader in middle school and high school who shared with me the struggles she had when growing up and who was open with me about challenges in her married life and who took me one-on-one to a number of different places just to hang out. She is someone who patterned for me what it means to go up to a young girl at church and take them out to do something.

I think of the women who I ran to when tired and emotionally exhausted who refueled my fire for Jesus by praying over me, hugging me, studying the Word with me, etc. (yes, you're included, Elaine), either over the phone or in person. I think of one woman who did a cooking class and a Bible study with me and a couple of others as a middle school student. I've cooked ever since.

I could tell you story after story of Barb, Elaine, Helen, Karen, Diane, Annette, Sigrid, etc., etc., and the list goes on and on. Their stories of their failings are so real, and yet I feel warmth when they open their lives to me and tell me how wonderful I am and how proud of me they are or simply when they just really listen and offer support by being an emotional cushion. This is what being a Christian is all about to me. It's about this deep need that only Christ's love and the love we have for each other can fill. I know I wouldn't be the missionary I am today without them. Where would I be without so many wonderful women of God who have backed me all these years? And don't even get me started on my mom!

Sue G (Age 61)

In my Coffee Break Bible Study, it was wonderful in my 40s to have a lesson each week with a woman who is now 102. Her sharing as a Bible study leader was a gentle blessing. How wonderful to have the Scriptures. The Holy Spirit would apply that individually to my heart to inspire and build me up. She was there, but I didn't have to get too personal if I didn't want to.

While being in an Al-Anon recovery group, I was blessed to have a sponsor (like a mentor) in my 50s who never judged me! She was one I could call on and get personal with when I was dealing with problems that came up that made me feel hurt, scared and angry, etc. What I found so helpful was that she put on her ears and listened. I found that to be the biggest help before ever hearing her say anything. Then she would share a similar experience and how she dealt with it and shared from the steps that are biblical. She never told me what to do but instead made suggestions on things that might help and what she did in a similar experience.

Then after talking with her, it would be good to ask the Lord what His answer was. I'm not sure I always did that, but I have learned that the Lord is faithful and nudges me in certain ways how to go about things that come up. Prayer is very important alongside listening to what others say. She is a Catholic, and I have been a blessing to her, and I pray for her needs too when they come up.

Through the years, as I have become less needy, we talk less, but we are still friends, and occasionally we chat to keep up with one another. Having her in my life has helped me from making some very big mistakes in my relationships and with my children and allowing them to grow up to take responsibility for themselves. The Lord used her in my life as a loving blessing with skin on! She was so patient and kind, and I thank God for her.

I now am sponsoring a gal in my town who is coming to the Lord gradually! She goes to church. I pray for her and ask the Lord to work Himself into her life. I am so thrilled that she wants to have and read a children's Bible at first and then later, as she gains more confidence, read the Bible. In time, maybe as she learns to trust me more, we can talk more about biblical things as I would love that, being a Coffee Break Bible Study leader.

Lorenna E (Age 30)

Having a mentor means that I get a window to see joys and challenges I may face as I get older. I've learned so much of who I want to be and who God is making me by watching mentors go before me. Sometimes their struggles and big steps of faith don't seem connected to my own life at all, but they offer me a window into God that I wouldn't be able to access on my own. Often I end up facing the very same experiences at a future date.

God sows seeds through my mentors, especially the ones I really open up to and who really open up to me, so that at a later date, those seeds help me walk through new circumstances with wisdom and grace. My faith grows when I see that God began preparing me years before for this very season, and He often chooses to do that through mentors. A loving, faith-filled mentor is crucial to growing in faith, love, peace and wisdom!

Deb A (Author of "There's No Place Like Home. A Journey of Faith, Hope and Love" Age 63)

When I was around 7-8 years young, I had an amazing woman, Mrs. Firchow, take me under her wings.

She would take me to the small Baptist church by her home for summer VBS. God gave her to me to be the godly woman who spoke affirmations into my life. When my mom would say horrible and ugly things to me that made me feel unwanted, Mrs. F. would say beautiful affirmations of loving, kind, encouraging words to me.

I believe in the many years I struggled with identity issues, I still remembered her kind and concerned words for someone else's child. I would encourage all mothers and grandmothers who see a child who doesn't have a person in their life that speaks affirmations of love and kindness to them to take them under your wings. Help them to know and understand that it wasn't God's plan that the words of others would hurt them. Protect them with your love and words from our Father who tells them they are beautiful. One day, they may turn to God for help to be rescued from this world. I did!

Emma S. (age 38)

I have had many women in my life who have helped shape me into who I am today. There are a few that stand out as mentors.

The first would be my Grandma Alice. When I was young, she taught me to bake, sew, clean, and work hard. Grandpa and Grandma would bring us to church every Sunday because that's what they did. They loved God, served Him, and that's how we show Him we love Him back. She also taught me so much by the way she lived her life more than by words. She loved me always, even when family relationships were strained later in life.

The next would be my Aunt. When I was 16, she reached out to me at a time in life I thought no one cared about me. Family life was rough, and she took me under her wing to teach me the basics of God. The seed that had been planted in my young life was watered.

Another woman came along when I was 16: my then boyfriend's (now husband) mother, Barb. She had three sons and always wanted a daughter. From the moment we started dating, that family treated me like part of theirs and even took my three younger siblings in from time to time. I am blessed to have a great relationship with my mother-in-law still today. She has given me so much of her wisdom about raising kids, being a good wife and mother-in-law.

There are so many other women who have impacted me over the years. I am so thankful and pray that I would one day also be a woman who impacts others for Christ Jesus.

My Mentor by Anita van der Elst (age 63)

I've always loved to read. The ability to read came early for me, even before I started going to school. One of my fave books as a child was a Bible story book. Hardbound in a navy blue, fabric-like cover, and about three inches thick, it provided coverage of Old Testament and New Testament Scripture in narrative form with a few color illustrations thrown in here and there. I read it several times. Sitting quietly in church for hours at a time posed no problem for me as long as I had something to read. The only thing available was my little KJV Bible so as young as age eight or nine, I was plowing through it, including all those major and minor prophets, and getting my mind boggled. The end result was familiarity with the stories, but not a whole lot of understanding.

Accepting Jesus as my Savior at age ten set me on a journey that continues to this day. But reading the Bible became a practice that mostly felt like a chore. I knew in my head that it was God's Word but didn't feel like it spoke to me personally, or that I could relate to it, or that it could affect my life in everyday practical ways.

Then along came Lois, a woman about twenty years older than I am. We met in a small church in Southern California when I was in my early forties. In getting to know her, we would talk about books we'd read and enjoyed. Then I found out that she had taken a course in Bible studies—the Bethel series, I think it was called. I asked her if it would be possible to get together on a one-on-one basis to talk about how to make the Bible personally applicable. She was delighted. Her advice to me was first to acknowledge the Holy Spirit's presence and invite His guidance, then to read with an open heart but a questioning mind. What was the setting of the part of the Bible I was reading? Who was speaking? Who was it written to or for? Why was this information included? What might it be like if I had been there at the time? How might I take what was there and apply it to my life? And if there was something that didn't make sense to me, make a note of it. She suggested I read from a variety of Bible versions and keep a journal of questions, "aha" moments and insights. We met a couple times a month to share a cup of tea and to go over anything I wanted to share from my journal and she would share of her vast store of biblical knowledge. This process brought life to my Bible reading and to my soul.

Lois also encouraged me to put myself into the scene of whatever unfolded on the page. Be one of the people in the crowd, or at the table, or in the battle. Maybe even write a story about it. A published author herself, she became my mentor in the area of writing as well. She led a writers' critiquing group that I was in for awhile, and we also met often one-on-one to talk about writing. It was through her that I had an opportunity to submit a devotional for a book compilation—and it was accepted.

We worked together on several writing projects and other areas of ministry at church over the years. Being mentored while serving on a team added another level and it came with a lasting friendship. Even though we live in different states now, we stay in touch, and I will always be grateful for her support and encouragement.

Gio (age 16)

There are many times in my life that I have felt like no one in this world understood me. I felt as if I was all alone in this cruel world and there wasn't anyone that I could fully trust. I came upon Launch Pad my 8th grade year and I started going out to a youth group at Sterry Memorial Church in Roswell. It was in January of 2015 when my life changed. I accepted Jesus Christ in my life and I have been very grateful since that day. I met some incredibly amazing people that are just as crazy for Jesus as I am. To this present day, I still face struggles because that's part of the everyday life, although I wouldn't be able to get through these obstacles without some of the most precious and great women that I have met along my path.

Growing up as a teen is challenging because you're figuring out who you are and what you want to be in life. For me, my life would not be the same without the advice and talks that I have with my mentors. Holly Kaiser is a huge role model to me. She is the youth group leader at Sterry. Because of her, I look at everything from a different perspective. My faith has grown more than I ever thought it could. I know that I and many others go out to her for help in times of need and she will always be there at any time. No matter what she has going on with her life, if you call her and need to talk, she will go out of her comfort zone for anyone. It is truly a blessing to have someone like Holly.

Seeing how passionate and loving Holly is towards the Lord gives me joy of knowing that there is a God who loves and forgives us for our mistakes. She taught me that it's okay to make mistakes, but never forget that the Lord will always be there for you. Of course, there are other wonderful women who help me out, but Holly is a special one. She was once a teen too and knows all about that stuff. The fact that I can count on her and know she will not judge me is awesome.

This world is full of temptation and it is really easy to fall into it. I know it is my own duty to grow in my faith, but I definitely would love to give a shout out to Holly for always giving me motivation to do my best and serve our Heavenly Father. I admire and aspire to be like her when I am older. I don't think I have ever and will ever encounter a time where I will be lost in my faith. Because I know my faith keeps growing every day and I know people like Holly are put in my life for a reason, to let me know that I am not alone.

Elaine Oostra

In the Same Way, Teach

TITUS 2:1-8

2 But what you teach must agree with true teaching.

²Tell the older men that in anything they do, they must not go too far. They must be worthy of respect. They must control themselves. They must have true faith. They must love others. They must not give up.

³ In the same way, teach the older women to lead a holy life. They must not tell lies about others. They must not let wine control them. Instead, they must teach what is good.

⁴ Then they can advise the younger women to love their husbands and children.

⁵ The younger women must control themselves and be pure. They must take good care of their homes. They must be kind. They must follow the lead of their husbands. Then no one will be able to speak evil things against God's word.

⁶ In the same way, help the young men to control themselves.

⁷ Do what is good. Set an example for them in everything. When you teach, be honest and serious.

⁸ No one can question the truth. So teach what is true. Then those who oppose you will be ashamed. That's because they will have nothing bad to say about us.

BIBLIOGRAPHY

"Agape" http://www.gotquestions.org/agape-love.html

"Confidence" http://www.biblestudytools.com/dictionary/confidence/
Orr, James, M.A., D.D. General Editor. "Entry for 'CONFIDENCE'". "International Standard Bible Encyclopedia". 1915   April 17,2017

"Covenant Marriage." http://covenantmarriage.com/what-is-a-marriage-covenant/
Copyright © 2017 Covenant Marriage Movement.   April 17,2017

"Covenant." http://www.biblestudytools.com/dictionary/covenant. Dictionaries - Baker's Evangelical Dictionary of Biblical Theology - Covenant   M.G. Easton M.A., D.D., Illustrated Bible Dictionary, Third Edition, published by Thomas Nelson, 1897   April 17,2017

"Definition of covenant" https://www.merriam-webster.com/dictionary/covenant© 2017 Merriam-Webster, Incorporated April 17,2017

"Eros" ThoughtCo   https://www.thoughtco.com/eros-romantic-love-in-the-bible-363367 April 17,2017

Got Questions.Org. "Can/should we interpret the bible as literal." © Copyright 2002-2017 Got Questions Ministries. *https://gotquestions.org/stay-at-home-mom.html* April 17, 2017

"God's Word to Women" http://www.godswordtowomen.org/submit.htm   Copyright © 2005 God's Word to Women   April 17, 2017

"[hahy-m*uh* n] hymen." http://www.dictionary.com/browse/hymen

"helper (Hb. 'ezer)" http://www.preceptaustin.org/hebrew_word_study_on_help#eze
Help - Hebrew Word Study. 08/20/2016   April 17,2017

"Insecure" http://www.dictionary.com/browse/insecure © 2017 Dictionary.com, LLC. April 17, 2017

"LOVE: A BIBLICAL PERSPECTIVE" http://www.biblestudymanuals.net/love.htm
Robertson's Word Pictures of the New Testament

http://bible.crosswalk.com/Commentaries/RobertsonsWordPictures/rwp.cgi? April 17, 2017

"Narcissistic" http://www.dictionary.com/browse/narcissistic © 2017 Dictionary.com, LLC.   April 17, 2017

"Perversion per·ver·sion."
https://www.bing.com/search?q=perverfsion&qs=n&form=QBRE&sp=-1&pq=perverfsion&sc=8-11&sk=&cvid=B3D845F414224B0A864780557A7AD107

April 17, 2017

"Phileō"
https://www.blueletterbible.org/lang/lexicon/lexicon.cfm?t=KJV&strongs=G5368 April 17, 2017

"Position Statement on Issues Related to Homosexuality." Scasta, David and Bialer, Philip. Authors. https://**www.psychiatry.org**/file library/about-apa/organization... PDF] April 17, 2017

"Reverence"   http://www.biblestudytools.com/dictionary/reverence/   April 17.2017

"Should all mothers be stay-at-home moms?" https://www.gotquestions.org/stay-at-home-mom.html   © Copyright 2002-2017 Got Questions Ministries   April 17, 2017

"SOUND'NESS, n." http://av1611.com/kjbp/kjv-dictionary/sound.html   The King James Bible Page   Webster's American Dictionary of the English Language, 1828. April 17, 2017

"Storge"   ThoughtCo   https://www.thoughtco.com/what-is-storge-love-700698

April 17, 2017

Strong's Concordance ishshah: woman, wife, female."
http://biblehub.com/hebrew/802.htm
© 2004 - 2016 by Bible Hub   April 17, 2017

"Why is virginity so important in the Bible?" https://www.gotquestions.org/Bible-virginity.html   © Copyright 2002-2017 Got Questions Ministries April 17, 2017

ABOUT THE AUTHOR

Elaine Oostra is the author of One Brick at a Time: Breaking Down Walls of Bitterness. She has studied the Bible for 20 years through Precept Ministries, an in-depth Bible class. It prepared her for what God had in store for her. Elaine is a speaker for women's groups. She serves in different youth ministries, including Launch Pad Ministries, a Christian release time class for middle and high school students. She has also served as a youth leader for nine years in her church. For the past 13 years, she has had, and continues to have, Bible studies in her home for high school girls. God has given her a passion and gift for teaching the youth.

Elaine has a passion for boldly teaching the uncompromising truths of the gospel. She desires for others to know God intimately and hunger for His Word, to then take the Word and share it with others. She desires for all believers to have discernment when a false gospel is being preached and to stand firm in God's Word.

Elaine and her husband have been married for 44 years (2017) and are self-employed farmers. They have four children, and four in-law (love) children, 16 grandchildren, 5 step grandchildren, and 1 great grandchild who are the delights of their hearts!

The joy of her heart is to see ALL come to a saving knowledge of Jesus Christ.

www.ingramcontent.com/pod-product-compliance
Lightning Source LLC
Chambersburg PA
CBHW081633040426
42449CB00014B/3285